MBUTI

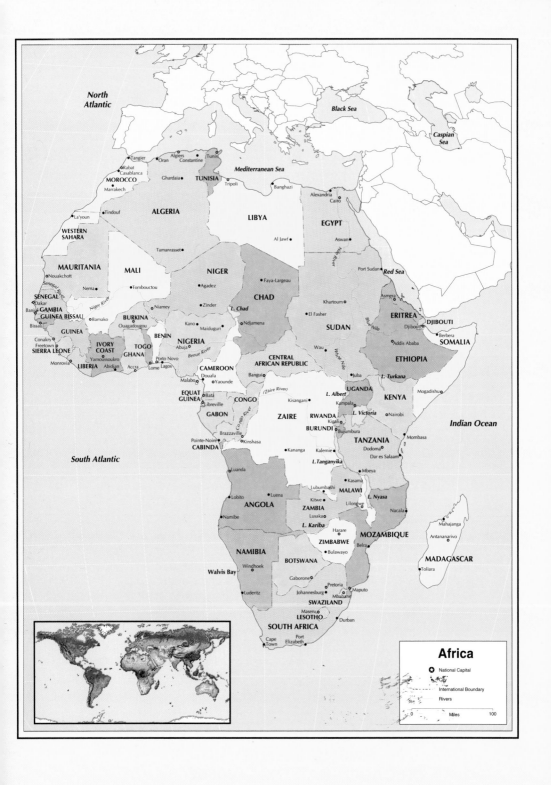

North
Atlantic

Black Sea

Caspian
Sea

Tangier
Algiers Tunis
Oran Constantine
Rabat
Casablanca
MOROCCO
Ghardaia
TUNISIA
Marrakech

Mediterranean Sea

Tripoli
Banghazi
Alexandria
Cairo

La'youn
Tindouf

ALGERIA

LIBYA

EGYPT

WESTERN
SAHARA

Al Jawf

Aswan

MAURITANIA

MALI

NIGER

Nile River

Port Sudan
Red Sea

Nouakchott

Nema

Tombouctou

Agadez

Faya-Largeau

Khartoum

Asmera

ERITREA

DJIBOUTI

SENEGAL
Dakar
GAMBIA
Banjul
GUINEA BISSAU
Bissau

Niger River

Niamey

Zinder

L. Chad

CHAD

Blue Nile

El Fasher

Djibouti

Berbera

SOMALIA

GUINEA
Conakry
Freetown
SIERRA LEONE
Monrovia
LIBERIA

BURKINA
Ouagadougou

Bamako

Kano
Maiduguri

Ndjamena

SUDAN

Wau

Addis Ababa

ETHIOPIA

IVORY
COAST
Yamoussoukro
Abidjan

TOGO
GHANA

BENIN

NIGERIA
Abuja

Benue River

CENTRAL
AFRICAN REPUBLIC

White Nile

Juba

L. Turkana

Mogadishu

Accra
Lome Lagos

Porto Novo

CAMEROON
Douala
Yaounde

Banqui

UGANDA

KENYA

EQUAT.
GUINEA
GABON

Bata
Libreville

CONGO

(Zaire River)

Kisangani

L. Albert

Kampala

Kigali

L. Victoria

Nairobi

Indian Ocean

South Atlantic

Pointe-Noire
CABINDA

Brazzaville
Kinshasa

ZAIRE

RWANDA
BURUNDI
Bujumbura

TANZANIA
Dodoma
Dar es Salaam

Mombasa

Kananga

Kalemie

L.Tanganyika

Mbeya

Luanda

Kasama

ANGOLA

Lobito

Luena

Lubumbashi

Kitwe

MALAWI

L. Nyasa

Namibe

ZAMBIA

Lusaka

Lilongwe

Nacala

L. Kariba

Harare

MOZAMBIQUE

Mahajanga

Antananarivo

ZIMBABWE

Belra

NAMIBIA

BOTSWANA

Bulawayo

MADAGASCAR

Walvis Bay

Windhoek

Toliara

Gaborone

Pretoria

Maputo

Luderitz

Johannesburg
Mbabane

SWAZILAND

Maseru
LESOTHO

SOUTH AFRICA

Cape
Town

Port
Elizabeth

Durban

Africa

National Capital

City

International Boundary

Rivers

0   Miles   100

MBUTI

Onukaba A. Ojo, Ph.D.

THE ROSEN PUBLISHING GROUP, INC.
NEW YORK

Published in 1996 by The Rosen Publishing Group, Inc.
29 East 21st Street, New York, NY 10010

First Edition

Manufactured in the United States of America

Library of Congress Cataloging-in-Publication Data

Adinoyi-Ojo, Onukaba, 1960–
    Mbuti / Onukaba A. Ojo. — 1st ed.
      p. cm. — (The heritage library of African peoples)
    Includes bibliographical references and index.
    ISBN 0-8239-1998-6
    1. Mbuti (African people)—Social life and customs—Juvenile
literature.   2. Ituri Forest (Zaire)—Social life and customs—
Juvenile literature. I. Title. II. Series.
DT650.B36A35   1995
305.896′394—dc20   94-22789
                                       CIP
                                       AC

Contents

INTRODUCTION

THERE IS EVERY REASON FOR US TO KNOW something about Africa and to understand its past and the way of life of its peoples. Africa is a rich continent that has for centuries provided the world with art, culture, labor, wealth, and natural resources. It has vast mineral deposits, fossil fuels, and commercial crops.

But perhaps most important is the fact that fossil evidence indicates that human beings originated in Africa. The earliest traces of human beings and their tools are almost two million years old. Their descendants have migrated throughout the world. To be human is to be of African descent.

The experiences of the peoples who stayed in Africa are as rich and as diverse as of those who established themselves elsewhere. This series of books describes their environment, their modes of subsistence, their relationships, and their customs and beliefs. The books present the variety of languages, histories, cultures, and religions that are to be found on the African continent. They demonstrate the historical linkages between African peoples and the way contemporary Africa has been affected by European colonial rule.

Africa is large, complex, and diverse. It encompasses an area of more than 11,700,000 square miles. The United States, Europe, and India could fit easily into it. The sheer size is an indication of the continent's great variety in geography, terrain, climate, flora, fauna, peoples, languages, and cultures.

Much of contemporary Africa has been shaped by European colonial rule, industrialization, urbanization, and the demands of a world economic system. For more than seventy years, large regions of Africa were ruled by Great Britain, France, Belgium, Portugal, and Spain. African peoples from various ethnic, linguistic, and cultural backgrounds were brought together to form colonial states.

For decades Africans struggled to gain their independence. It was not until after World War II that the colonial territories become independent African states. Today, almost all of Africa is ruled by Africans. Large numbers of Africans live in modern cities. Rural Africa is also being transformed, and yet its people still engage in many of their age-old customs and beliefs.

Contemporary circumstances and natural events have not always been kind to ordinary Africans. Today, however, new popular social movements and technological innovations pose great promise for future development.

George C. Bond, Ph.D., Director
Institute of African Studies
Columbia University, New York

Nomadic groups of hunters and gatherers, the Mbuti live in the Ituri forest in Zaire.

chapter

1

THE MBUTI

THE MBUTI ARE NOMADIC GROUPS OF hunters and gatherers who live in small temporary camps in the southern and central parts of the dense Ituri rain forest in Zaire, central Africa. They frequently move camp to reap the benefit of new areas of the forest nearby. Today, they have also established reciprocal relationships with settled African peoples in villages close to the forest. Their population is estimated at 20,000 to 50,000, scattered all over the vast forest. They have been celebrated worldwide in books, films, sculptures, and drawings both for their durability and for their physique.

The average Mbuti adult is often no more than four feet, six inches tall. Some call them Pygmies. They call themselves Bambuti (the Mbuti people). The term "Pygmy" often carries negative connotations, as if the relative shortness

Map showing location of the Mbuti people in the Ituri rainforest of northeastern Zaire.

of a group of people were a disability. The Mbuti are normal human beings. Perhaps because of constant ridicule from their much taller neighbors, the Mbuti have grown acutely sensitive to slights. It is said that in the past when a Mbuti met a non-Mbuti along the way, he would ask when the other first saw him. If the non-Mbuti confessed having just seen him, the Mbuti would feel insulted and might even fight: The non-Mbuti was implying that the Mbuti are so short that they can be seen only at close range. If, on the other hand, the non-

Mbuti claimed to have sighted him from afar, the Mbuti would be friendly and pleasant.

Western scientists have for years speculated on why the Mbuti are so short in stature. The explanations suggested include scarcity of highly nourishing food; a genetic condition attributed to inbreeding, natural selection, and adaptation to the forest environment; a growth-hormone deficiency, and the inadequacy of a substance identified as crucial to growth in human beings.

We may never know the answer to this puzzle. What is important is that the Mbuti do not feel handicapped by their height. In fact, they are able to move around in the dark, complex forest with relative ease and agility precisely because of their height. Where taller people stoop or crawl, the Mbuti slip through effortlessly.

▼ WAY OF LIFE ▼

The Mbuti sleep in small one-room, beehive-shaped shelters made out of saplings and leaves. Each shelter has one tiny opening. There are no windows. A hut can be built in less than two hours. It is neither high enough for an adult to stand up in nor wide enough for an adult to lie down at full length. To be able to sleep inside it, an adult must curl up. Separate shelters are built for married people and for boys and girls.

Because the Mbuti are nomadic, they have no need for permanent dwellings. The shelters they sleep in can be built within two hours.

As nomads, the Mbuti have seen no need for more lasting and comfortable homes. They generally move almost every month, adapting themselves easily to a location nearby.

The traditional garment of the Mbuti is a narrow strip of bark cloth worn like a G-string by both men and women, old and young. The rest of the body is uncovered. This style is of course dictated by the environment. The Mbuti live in a hot, humid tropical forest. Most Mbuti go barefooted. Shoes are too noisy when game is being stalked. A barefooted hunter stepping on dry leaves makes less noise than one with shoes.

▼ THE CAMP ▼

As a people, the Mbuti are now widely scattered. They live in isolated groups with ten to twenty-five families in each camp. They have all but lost their own language through this way of life. Today, each band tends to adopt the language of the neighboring villages with which they have forged economic and cultural links. Most Mbuti speak Bira, adopted from the neighboring Bira villages, as well as the regional lingua franca, KiNgwana. This is a fusion of Arabic and indigenous African languages that evolved during the slave trade.

▼ THE SLAVE TRADE ▼

Lasting from the early sixteenth until the late nineteenth century, the slave trade was the business of obtaining human beings mostly from Africa for sale in Europe and the Americas. During its 400 years, millions of Africans were captured and sold into servitude. This global business was run by Arabs, Europeans, Americans, and their African agents. The slaves were chained and shipped under inhuman conditions across the Atlantic and Indian Oceans, to be resold mostly to owners of sugar, tobacco, and cotton plantations in the West Indies and in North and South America. There most of them toiled for their owners till death. Some escaped to freedom elsewhere, and some worked

The density of the forest surrounding the Mbuti helped protect them from falling victim to slave raids.

and raised enough money to pay for their freedom.

To maintain a steady supply of slaves in those days, African towns and villages were constantly raided and plundered by the slave merchants and their paid agents in search of people to capture. The impenetrable Ituri forest protected the Mbuti from these raids. As a result, only a few of them were ever taken as slaves.

One Mbuti who did see North America was the tragically famous Ota Benga, who was lured from the Ituri forest in the early 1900s by Samuel Phillips Verner, a white missionary from South Carolina. Ota Benga was exhibited at the

St. Louis World's Fair in 1904 with other so called "strange people." He was later taken to the Bronx Zoo in New York and put in a cage with orangutans in a bizarre experiment proposed by racist scientists who hoped to learn what he had in common with animals. Abused and humiliated all over the United States, Ota Benga committed suicide in Lynchburg, Virginia, in 1914. Two years ago, his tragic story was the subject of a penetrating biography, *Ota Benga: The Pygmy in the Zoo*, written by Verner's grandson, Phillips Verner Bradford, and Harvey Blume.

▼ OTHER PEOPLES ▼

The Mbuti share the Ituri forest with other groups of short, nomadic people. The Efe occupy the northern and northeastern parts of the forest. They have adopted the languages of the neighboring Lese and Mamvu villages and enjoy close economic and social ties with them. Most Mbuti hunters use nets woven with twine from *kusa* vine. The Efe use mostly bows and wooden-tipped arrows. But both groups use spears.

Besides the Mbuti and Efe, the Ituri forest is home to two other less populous groups of migratory hunters and gatherers known as the Aka and Sua. They associate with the Mangbetu and Budu villages and speak their languages.

The Mbuti share the Ituri forest with several other nomadic peoples. One of these groups, the Aka, are also hunters and gatherers. They, too, hold their children in high esteem.

In the neighboring nation of Congo, about 1,000 miles west of the Ituri forest, live the Bayaka, part of the Bambuti group. All these groups—Mbuti, Efe, Aka, Sua, and Bayaka—speak KiNgwana in addition to the languages of the villages with which they are associated.▲

2

THE ITURI RAIN FOREST

THE ITURI FOREST LIES HALF A DEGREE NORTH of the Equator in the central African nation of Zaire. The forest is about 50,000 square miles in area, roughly the size of New York State. A narrow dirt road runs through it from east to west. The road was built on the route that had been used during the 1800s by Arab and Western merchants for the movement of slaves and ivories to the Atlantic coast some 1,500 miles away. It is possible to travel for hundreds of miles in this dense forest without seeing the sun.

The Ituri forest is to the Mbuti what the Arctic is to the Inuit ("Eskimo"). They live in it and from it. In fact, the Mbuti call themselves *Ba miki ba ndula*, "Children of the forest." The forest is indeed generous to the Mbuti. They move freely all over its vast expanse, foraging for food such as wild animals, fruits, vegetables,

...dies have shown that hunter/gatherer societies fulfill their needs (finding food, drink, shelter, ...c) quicker than any other peoples. Their efficiency and speed allows them much leisure time.

The Mbuti call themselves *Ba miki ba ndula,* "Children of the forest."

mushrooms, and honey, and for drinking water and the firewood with which they cook their food, warm themselves, and illuminate their camps. The forest also gives them free shelter, free clothing, and security from hostile peoples and unwelcome ideas.

Modern social amenities do not exist, and the Mbuti have no strong desire for such things because they have never been part of their daily lives.

Occupying two-fifths of Zaire, the Ituri is made up of tall, broad-leafed evergreen trees. Most of the trees range from 100 to 200 feet in height. The forest ground is moist and cool all

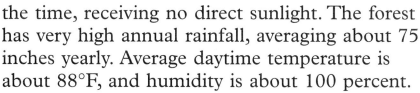

the time, receiving no direct sunlight. The forest has very high annual rainfall, averaging about 75 inches yearly. Average daytime temperature is about 88°F, and humidity is about 100 percent.

Among the animals commonly found in the forest are okapis, antelopes, duikers, buffaloes, elephants, leopards, forest hogs, peacocks, monkeys, snakes, and rabbits. These animals are hunted by the Mbuti both for their own consumption and for sale to neighboring villagers.▲

chapter

3

THE SOCIAL SYSTEM

THE SOCIAL STRUCTURE OF ANY GROUP OF people is the way in which all the different components of the group are organized and interrelated. In this chapter, we shall look at the Mbuti worldview or beliefs, the pattern of relationships among its members, and the nature of such Mbuti institutions as family, marriage, government, and education.

▼ KINSHIP ▼

Mbuti camps are usually made up of closely related families. Kinship among Mbuti can be broadly categorized into parents, siblings, couples, cousins, and in-laws. Outsiders are rare in a camp. Age is greatly valued and respected. The young ones refer to every elderly person as either *eba* (father) or *ema* (mother). They are expected to obey and serve such an elder just as

Children are cared for by the entire Mbuti camp.

they would their own parents. The elders too treat the young ones like their own, punishing or correcting them when they do wrong, and commending or rewarding them for being good.

As a result of these strong kinship ties, there are no orphans, no abandoned children, no childless mothers, and no lonely children or lonely old people in any Mbuti camp. Several women are at hand to breast-feed, clean, wash, and comfort children whose biological mothers are temporarily unavailable or have died. Childless women have so many children to take care of that they forget their private pains. Old people are also looked after by the community.

Each person in an Mbuti camp has a role in making the camp function. For these two older Mbuti, it means sifting the manioc which will be used for meals at a later time.

No child or elderly person is ever alone or lonely, for he or she is always constantly sur-rounded by people.

The Mbuti society is a patrilinear one, which means that descent is traced through the male line. Since the Mbuti generally have few posses-sions to pass on after death to their children, patriliny offers the men no significant advantage over the women.

▼ MARRIAGE ▼

Like most people, the hope of the average Mbuti is to marry, have children, and live a long and happy life together. Couples tend to have many children. The approval of both sets of parents is usually sought before marriages take place. The would-be groom kills an antelope and offers it to the father of the woman as a bride price. It is not a payment for the woman; it is merely a gesture of appreciation to the family of the woman.

After the marriage, the couple are expected to raise their own shelter and live in it together. Marriages are generally monogamous. Divorces are few. Forced marriages are rare. Women choose their own husbands. Since each camp is often inhabited mostly by blood relations, eligible young women in one camp usually marry eligible men in other camps.

Unmarried Mbuti youths enjoy much sexual

In addition to domestic work, Mbuti women also gather food in the baskets they've made for that purpose.

freedom. They practice *arobo* or free love. Youth is considered the period of experimentation and exploration. Young people are, therefore, given the chance to find out things on their own, to satisfy their curiosity, and to prepare themselves for the future. Despite premarital permissiveness, the Mbuti seldom have children outside of marriage.

▼ SOCIAL ROLES ▼

Mbuti women do most of the domestic chores. These include cooking and serving meals, cleaning, washing, fetching drinking water from nearby streams or rivers, collecting firewood, and looking after the children. It is also the women who weave the baskets used in

The bark cloth worn by both Mbuti men and women is made by the men and dyed by the women.

food gathering in the forest. But hunting nets, spears, and bows and arrows are made and repaired by men. The bark cloth worn by the Mbuti is also made by the men. They cut the bark from the right tree and strip off the hard outer coverings, leaving the softer inner layer to be pounded into a fibrous cloth. The Mbuti women decorate these cloths using a vegetable dye.

These designs on bark cloth by Mbuti women have been acclaimed as a unique art form. In August 1991, the Margo Leavin Gallery in Los Angeles, California, exhibited 51 such pigment drawings on bark cloth by Mbuti women. They were lavishly praised by the arts community. The

27

The Mbuti do not segregate social roles by sex. Both men and women are responsible for hunting and gathering. To the left, an Mbuti woman sets a net. Below, an Mbuti man hunts with bow and arrow.

Mbuti did not, of course, create the cloths for exhibition. They were made to be used and discarded when they become too old and ragged.

The strict segregation of social roles on the domestic front is absent when it comes to obtaining food. Hunting and gathering are done by both Mbuti men and women. Together they set the nets, drive the animals into them, and kill them with spears and arrows. They pick mushrooms, fruits, vegetables, and nuts together. The killing of such powerful animals as elephants, leopards, and forest hogs—as well as the often difficult task of picking honey combs—is usually done by men.

▼ POLITICAL LEADERSHIP ▼

Because they are few in number, isolated, and nomadic, the Mbuti do not have a strong central political authority or a distinct and powerful leader or ruler. Most decisions are taken by consensus. There are no legislatures, courts, or presidency. It is a society without police or an army, air, or naval forces. It has no newspaper or magazine, no radio or television station.

Mbuti youths play important political roles in the camp because the elders consider them the owners of the future. They make many key decisions on behalf of the group. They are the singers, the dancers, and the drummers. They decide when and how the communal religious and cultural ceremonies are to be performed.

Through these performances, they are able to critique the actions of adults and elderly members of the community. In these performances they exercise a license to ridicule, parody, and protest any antisocial behavior or improper conduct by the adults.

▼ WORLDVIEW ▼

The Mbuti regard the forest as sacred. They believe in the existence of a benevolent deity that lives at the center of the forest and controls everything within it. This forest deity is considered to be the giver of life (whether plant life or animal life), and of consciousness.

The Mbuti constantly strive for balance and harmony between themselves and this guardian deity. They sing, dance, drum, and mime for it, trying to honor and thank it for giving them shelter, food, clothing, warmth, and love. They call the deity their "father" or their "mother" in much the same way that other organized religions use terms of endearment in reverence of their divinities.

They consider themselves to be part of their natural environment. Unlike the West, which often views nature and culture as opposites, the Mbuti treat the two as an integrated entity.

Traditionally, the Mbuti attach little value

The Mbuti often take their drums to nearby villages to sing and dance with their neighbors.

Women dance in an Epulu village.

Like other African cultures, the Mbuti consider filed teeth to be beautiful.

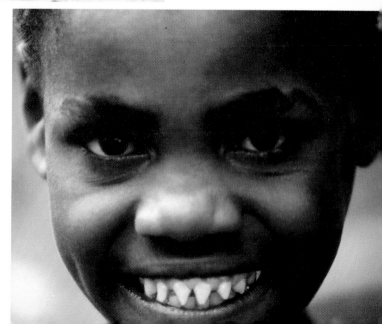

to material wealth because it is perishable and renewable. Because of the way they live, it is impossible to accumulate property. There are therefore no rich or poor people within any Mbuti group. Most things are communally owned. Moral values are treasured much more than material goods.

▼ EDUCATION ▼

The Mbuti are socialized from infancy to imbibe the values of sharing, egalitarianism, community, and cooperation. As soon as they are able to play on their own, children join the *bopi*, the communal playground. There they mix, play (mostly tree-climbing), and learn about life and the society from their age mates and from older children.

Children are often left behind at the camp with Mbuti elders while their parents are out hunting and gathering. These old men and women instruct the children on their rights and responsibilities. The elders enact mimes in which they play the animals in the forest and show the children how to trap and kill them. Through such mimes the children learn how to hunt with nets, spears, and bows and arrows. They are also taught how to light fires, weave and repair nets, and make and maintain bows and arrows.▲

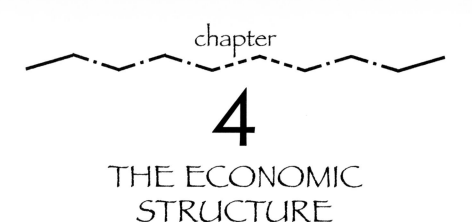

chapter

4

THE ECONOMIC
STRUCTURE

THE MBUTI DO NOT CULTIVATE CROPS EITHER
for their own consumption or for sale to other
people. They also do not domesticate animals.
They survive mainly on the game they kill and
on the food they gather from the forest.

They trade their meat surpluses with the
neighboring villagers, who grow such food as
manioc, banana, plantain, sweet potatoes, pea-
nuts, and pineapples, which are also consumed
by the Mbuti.

Besides meat protein, the Mbuti also supply
the villagers with animal hides, feathers, ivories,
saplings and leaves for building their dwellings,
and bark for clothing. From the villagers, the
Mbuti obtain iron tools such as knives, spears,
iron-tipped arrows, and cooking pots, water
buckets, or bowls.

Hunting is limited to about four hours a day,

The Mbuti hunt for about four hours a day, five days a week.

five days a week. The rest of their time is spent on leisure, communal ceremonies, domestic chores, production and maintenance of tools, and visits to the neighboring villages to sell their meat or to partake in social activities.

The area to be hunted is chosen by consensus the evening before. The Mbuti are able to determine where the game is by monitoring animal tracks, scent, dung or droppings, fallen hair or feathers, or cast-off skins. The hunting band sets out for the site early in the day. On arrival, the area is cordoned off, and the nets are set up at strategic points. This preparation is done in relative silence to avoid alerting the animals before the nets are ready.

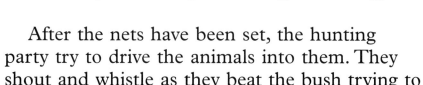

After the nets have been set, the hunting party try to drive the animals into them. They shout and whistle as they beat the bush trying to scare the animals into the nets. Animals not trapped by the nets are either caught with bare hands or shot with bows and arrows and spears by those who have been positioned for this task.

The Mbuti have long understood the need for conservation. They created a sanctuary in the middle of the Ituri forest. Hunting is forbidden in that part of the forest, which also happens to be the residence of Mbuti's guardian deity. A limit on the number of hours and days in which hunting can be done is also part of their conservation strategy.▲

chapter

5

CULTURAL AND RELIGIOUS PRACTICES

CULTURE IS THE SUM TOTAL OF THE WAYS IN which a group of people live. It includes their beliefs, behaviors, language, and religious and secular celebrations, as well as various forms of expression such as music, painting, sculpture, dance, film, and mime.

Like many other societies in Africa, the Mbuti have a rich repertoire of cultural and religious ceremonies. These ceremonies serve to define and distinguish the Mbuti as a unique group of people. They also entertain the people, honor the guardian spirit of the forest, reinforce communal values, and reaffirm the Mbuti's past.

The Mbuti celebrate the following: *Elima,* a puberty and initiation rite for women; *Molimo,* a purification ceremony performed mostly by men; *Nkumbi,* a circumcision and initiation ceremony for men; and *Ekokomea,* an erotic dance

The Mbuti are great storytellers, often using mime and gesture to emphasize or describe events.

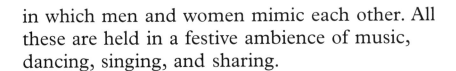

in which men and women mimic each other. All these are held in a festive ambience of music, dancing, singing, and sharing.

▼ *ELIMA* ▼

Elima celebrates Mbuti girls' transition from puberty to adulthood. The festival is held at the camp shortly after a young woman's first menstrual period. Before the festival, the initiate is secluded in a shelter and taught the values of her society as well as the responsibilities and challenges of womanhood.

On the day of the festival, the initiate emerges from seclusion accompanied by her friends. They sing and dance in a circle to music supplied by the men. The festival is often well attended by the camp's eligible bachelors.

If a woman likes a man, she shows it by playfully hitting him with a stick. Later that night, the lucky man spends the night with the woman in her shelter. But he can be prevented from going into the shelter by other women. He has to fight his way through the human barrier to reach the woman. The ordeal is meant to test his strength, persistence, toughness, and ability to survive the trials of life.

Elima often includes a tug-of-war between men and women. The objective is not to produce a winning side but merely to entertain the participants.

One form of recreation among the Mbuti is smoking a banana leaf stem. The man sits on a traditional Mbuti chair made of four sticks balanced together.

▼ MOLIMO ▼

Molimo is a ceremony performed at a camp when there is a crisis such as the death of an esteemed member of the camp, bad hunting, illness, or a moral transgression (adultery, theft, greed, and so on). It is held, usually in a rainless period, to cleanse the forest and appease the guardian deity. Sometimes *Molimo* is performed by Mbuti youths as a critique and a parody of adult follies and antisocial behavior. It can last for as long as one month. Men organize and control *Molimo*.

The *Molimo* symbol is a sacred trumpet. It is hidden in the bush away from women and children, who must not know that a trumpet produces *Molimo*'s trademark sound. The *Molimo* begins at the sound of the trumpet. Upon hearing the sound, women and children must go into their shelters. The trumpet is blown several times round the camp. When it stops, the women and children reemerge from the shelters to join the men. Together, they dance and sing around a big fire that has been built at the center of the camp. The *mangese*, men and women too old to participate, sit and watch the performers.

In the past, women and children were required to stay indoors for an entire *Molimo* night, leaving the men to eat food prepared by the women and sing and dance for the forest deity. Nowadays, women and children are expected to go into their shelters only while the trumpet is being brought into the camp.

From the bush on the outskirts of the camp, the *Molimo* trumpet sings a familiar tune and mimics animal sounds. In the camp, the drummers respond with the appropriate beat. At first, the men hum the song, then sing it, their eyes firmly fixed on the fire. Sometimes, the trumpet leads the song and the men chorus it. At other times, the men raise the song and the trumpet echoes it.

This call-and-response goes on for a while. The hunters with the sacred trumpet then emerge from the bush, circle the fire with the trumpet, and then lay it on the ground for one of the old men to rub it with ashes from the sacred fire. The trumpet is a six-foot long, three-inch wide blackened bamboo stem.

As soon as the trumpet has been anointed by the elder, its bearers pick it up and disappear into the forest again, taking messages of goodwill from the people to the forest deity.

With the trumpet gone, the women and children return to dance, sing, and feast with the men. At some point in the performance, the women tie up the men, symbolically silencing them and assuming control of both the ceremony and of the land. The men must beg and pay the women a ransom to be freed from cap-

tivity. This is meant to teach the men the limit of their power and affirm the strength and influence of the women as a group.

When *Molimo* is performed as a critique or to protest certain actions of the adult members of the camp, the trumpet does not sing but mimics the cries of such dangerous animals as the elephant and the leopard. The objective of the young performers is to terrify the adult offenders. During this kind of *Molimo*, the trumpet-bearers come into the camp and destroy things to signify the youths' displeasure or anger amidst protests and threats from the adults.

▼ *EKOKOMEA* ▼

Ekokomea is an erotic dance in which men and women mimic each other. Women dance with logs between their legs, making sport of men's maleness. The men pretend to be washing their private parts, parodying women.

▼ *NKUMBI* ▼

The *Nkumbi* is a three-month boys' initiation ceremony that the Mbuti celebrate jointly with the neighboring villages. It is held in a village square every three years to purify both the villages and the forest. Before the ceremony, the initiates are secluded and taught the history and moral values of the two communities. They

The tattoos on an Mbuti man's chest and back signify that he has been through *Nkumbi*, a three-month initiation ceremony.

emerge from seclusion to a festival of songs, dance, and music. Boys are circumcised during the ceremony. All the initiates are tattooed on the chest and back, signifying their passage from boyhood into adulthood and their membership in the *Nkumbi* initiation group.▲

6

THE MBUTI AND THEIR NEIGHBORS

THE MBUTI HAVE A SYMBIOTIC RELATIONSHIP with the taller villagers who live at the periphery of the Ituri forest. The villagers depend on the Mbuti for their meat, and the Mbuti obtain cultivated food, iron tools, and weapons from them. The villagers are immigrants to the region who have settled permanently along the lone narrow dirt road that runs through the forest. They are mostly farmers and fishermen. They seldom venture deep into the forest, fearing that they might be attacked by the evil spirits that they believe dwell in it.

Each Mbuti family attaches itself to a family in the village called *kpara* or "patron." Nowadays with the Mbuti increasingly spending more time in the villages, it perhaps makes sense to create stronger ties with the villagers. The Mbuti are more accustomed to the forest than to life in

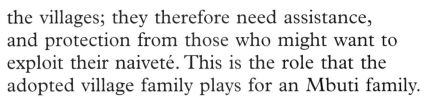

the villages; they therefore need assistance, and protection from those who might want to exploit their naiveté. This is the role that the adopted village family plays for an Mbuti family.

Marriages between Mbuti and the villagers are common, but the exchange is often one-sided. The men from the villages like to have Mbuti women as wives because of their loyalty and hard work, but the village women seldom marry Mbuti men. There is a subtle discrimination against the Mbuti because of their physique.

▼ GOVERNMENT INTERVENTION ▼

Worried that the villagers were mistreating and exploiting the Mbuti, the government of Mobutu Sese Seko, President of Zaire since 1965, adopted some measures in the late 1960s and early 1970s to protect the Mbuti. The government pronounced them full citizens of Zaire, entitled to the same rights as everyone else in the country. An affirmative action program was undertaken to redress the alleged injustices (such as the subtle discrimination and the perceived exploitative relationship) against the Mbuti. Any Mbuti, for instance, who wished to abandon the forest and settle in the villages was given free housing, clothing, and farming tools and seeds.

As a result of this preferential treatment, the

Concerned with the potential mistreatment of the Mbuti by neighboring peoples, the government has declared the Mbuti full citizens of Zaire, granting them the same rights as all other citizens. Mbuti children grow up protected, and also restricted, by the laws

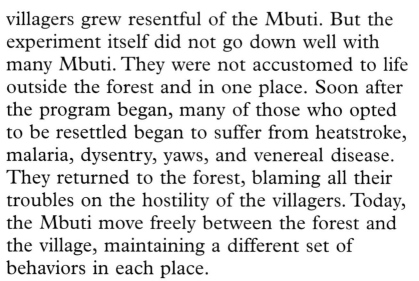

villagers grew resentful of the Mbuti. But the experiment itself did not go down well with many Mbuti. They were not accustomed to life outside the forest and in one place. Soon after the program began, many of those who opted to be resettled began to suffer from heatstroke, malaria, dysentry, yaws, and venereal disease. They returned to the forest, blaming all their troubles on the hostility of the villagers. Today, the Mbuti move freely between the forest and the village, maintaining a different set of behaviors in each place.

The construction of a dirt road through the forest attracted more people to the area, including government officials, soldiers, shopkeepers, road workers, drivers, government clerks, etc. Social facilities such as canteens, bars, and stores opened up along the road.

With the increase in the roadside population came demand on the Mbuti to bring more supplies from the forest. In order to meet this demand, the Mbuti began to kill more game than they actually needed for survival.▲

The road built through the Ituri forest has brought some unwelcome guests to the people of the forest over the last two centuries.

chapter

7

SOCIAL CHANGE

FOR THOUSANDS OF YEARS, THE IMPENETRABLE
Ituri forest shielded the Mbuti from the rapid
changes taking place all around them. But
with increased contacts between them and the
growing village population, some fundamental
changes are beginning to be noticed in the
Mbuti way of life.

An earlier source of change came with the
Arab slave traders around the 18th century.
They were the first foreigners to arrive in the
region, looking for slaves, ivory, and spices to
sell to European and American merchants. The
most notorious of the Arab slave traders was
Tippu Tib, whom Henry M. Stanley met at
various times during his trips to the area in the
late 19th century. Before the Arabs were eventu-
ally dislodged from the region by the Europeans,
they had mixed and intermarried with many

African communities on their slave route. This racial mixture produced in the region a group known as *Ngwana,* a flourishing mixed language called KiNgwana, and the introduction of the Islamic religion. As a result of contact with this group of Africans who had been heavily influenced by Arabs, the Mbuti picked up KiNgwana, which grew over time to become the lingua franca in the region.

▼ BELGIAN INFLUENCE ▼

Like the Arab influence, Belgian colonialism did not impact directly on the Mbuti. Foreign influences were, in most cases, felt first by the villagers who lived along the road. Through contact with these villagers, the Mbuti began to pick up bits and pieces of this new life.

Henry M. Stanley is usually identified as having opened the region to Western exploitation. Stanley first visited the region as a correspondent of the now defunct *New York Herald,* to rescue Dr. David Livingstone, a Scottish missionary and explorer who had come to Africa in 1866 to look for the source of the Nile River. Stanley found Livingstone in 1871, and his reports of their encounter as well as his writings on his experiences during that and subsequent trips to Africa earned him fame in the West. It was these writings that interested the Belgian king, Leopold II, in this part of central Africa.

The Mbuti managed to avoid much of the devastation wrought in central Africa by King Leopold of Belgium.

Leopold later hired Stanley to pave the way for him to establish his authority and ownership over the region. Stanley set up stations in the area and negotiated dubious treaties with illiterate local rulers. His journeys throughout the region were marked by violence and brutality against Africans. Thousands of Africans were forced to work for him without pay, and thousands more were massacred on suspicion of hostility toward Stanley and his entourage as they stomped through the land, pillaging and plundering everything the people held dear. He was severely criticized in the West for his brutality, forcefulness, and mercenary approach. Because of his lack of restraint while pushing his way through the forest, the Africans nicknamed him *Bula Matari,* meaning "Breaker of Rocks."

Leopold took over the area in 1884 and named it the "Congo Free State." It was run as his private property. His administration was perhaps the worst in the history of colonialism. His agents beat, mutilated, and executed millions of Africans in the quest for rubber and ivory. Liberal-minded Westerners were outraged by these gross abuses.

Leopold was forced in 1908 to transfer the state to the Belgian government to be adminis-tered as a colonial territory known as the Belgian Congo. The population of the territory declined from about 30 million in 1884, when Leopold took over, to less than 8 million at the end of his rule in 1908. The drop was attributed by independent researchers to the terror and havoc that were unleashed by Stanley and others working for Leopold as well as to disease, famine, and the physical and social disruption caused by the imperial enterprise.

Again, because of the security offered by the forest, most Mbuti did not experience these horrors. The Mbuti encountered this murderous gang of foreigners only when they ventured near the road or the villages. Stanley and his entou-rage ran into a few Mbuti on the road and con-scripted them as guides through the forest and to teach them how to survive in it. A few others fell into the hands of Leopold's men and were forced to work for them. But by and large, the majority of Mbuti were shielded from the harshness of colonial life. The more vulnerable villagers began to appropriate certain aspects of Western life and culture through such institutions as schools, churches, and government. The Mbuti exposed themselves to these Western values while in the villages. Today, there are Western-educated Mbuti, and Western goods, clothes, and food can sometimes be found among them.

The Mbuti were not the only people in the Ituri forest in periods of national crisis. At the height of the struggle for independence from Belgium in the 1950s, some of the freedom fighters slipped into the forest to evade their Belgian pursuers. As hosts, the Mbuti took care of these people, sharing food, shelter, and news about the world of the forest and the political situation in the world outside it.

Independence came on June 30, 1960, with Patrice Lumumba as the first African Prime Minister of the new nation. Because the Belgians had not prepared the country adequately for self-rule, Belgian Congo—which would later be known as Zaire—was soon thrown into political turmoil. Lumumba was assassinated. A region of the country wanted to secede. An international effort to hold the country together worked only for a while. A military coup led by

Today, as with many other African peoples, there are Western-educated Mbuti.

Mobutu Sese Seko was announced in 1965. It took the Mobutu government at least five years to restore peace. The country was renamed Zaire in 1971.

During the political upheavals of the 1960s, many of the villagers escaped into the forest, taking with them their own values and material goods, which they shared with their hosts, the Mbuti, in exchange for Mbuti hospitality and guidance.

By the time the villagers returned to their villages after the war, the Mbuti had adopted some of their values and lifestyle. Today, the Mbuti have partially embraced such alien concepts as hierarchy, independence, competition, and the use and misuse of money as a medium of exchange. Also, some Mbuti cultural and religious practices were incorporated into those of the villagers. For instance, *Nkumbi*, the male initiation ceremony, is now jointly celebrated by the Mbuti and the villagers.

The Zairean government tried unsuccessfully to persuade the Mbuti to change their ways of life. The government wanted them to farm or do other more productive work to make their contribution to the new nation. As hunters and gatherers, their income could not easily be assessed for taxes. Many tax collectors would not venture into the deep forest to make the Mbuti pay.

Despite attempts by the Zairean government to get the Mbuti to farm or do other work considered more "productive," the Mbuti have successfully maintained many of their traditional ways.

The government built a National Park at Epulu, the southern part of the forest. The Park authorities tried in vain to curtail or ban the Mbuti from hunting in the area. Not that the Park authorities were motivated by any noble goals. The Park was itself thriving on capturing and selling animals to foreign zoos. A number of Mbuti were employed in the Park as guides because of their extensive knowledge of the forest.

To the few Christian mission schools in the region, the Zairean government added several more. At first, many Mbuti flocked to these schools out of sheer curiosity. Nowadays, more

The economy of Zaire is dependent, in part, on trade along the Zaire River. Young Mbuti men and women have joined in supporting the national and local economies by taking advantage of their access to the river and the resources provided by the forest.

and more Mbuti are receiving Western education. Many of these people are not likely to return to a life of hunting and gathering in the forest.▲

Glossary

Aka Group of diminutive migratory hunters and gatherers associated with the Mangbetu and Budu villagers.

Bayaka Group of diminutive migratory hunters and gatherers in Congo.

Bira The villagers with whom the Mbuti are mostly associated.

bopi The communal children's playground.

Budu A group of villagers associated with the Aka and Sua.

eba Father.

Efe A group of diminutive migratory hunters and gatherers associated with the Lese and Mamvu villagers.

Ekokomea An Mbuti erotic dance in which men and women mimic each other.

Elima The girls' initiation and puberty rite.

ema Mother.

kpara Patron.

KiNgwana The lingua franca of the Ituri region.

Lese A group of villagers associated with the Efe.

lingua franca A language that is widely used as a means of communication among peoples with different languages.

Mamvu A group of villagers associated with the Efe.

Mangbetu A group of villagers associated with the Aka and Sua.

miki Child.

Molimo Purification ritual symbolized by a sacred trumpet.

Nkubi An initiation ceremony for boys celebrated by the Mbuti with their neighboring villages.

Sua A group of diminutive migratory hunters and gatherers associated with the Mangbetu and Budu villagers.

For Further Reading

Bradford, Phillips Verner, and Blume, Harvey. *Ota Benga: The Pygmy in the Zoo*. New York: St. Martin's Press, 1992.

Duffy, Kevin. *Children of the Forest*. New York: Dodd, Mead and Co., 1984.

Challenging Reading

Nurit Bird-David. "Beyond 'The Original Affluent Society'": A Culturalist Reformation." In *Current Anthropology*, vol. 33, No. 1 February, 1992.

Turnbull, Colin M. *The Mbuti Pygmies: Change and Adaptation*. New York: CBS College Publishing, 1983.

———. *Wayward Servants: The Two Worlds of the African Pygmies*. Garden City, NY: American Museum of Natural History, 1965.

———. *The Forest People*. New York: Simon and Schuster, 1961.

Wilkie, David S., and Curran, Bryan. "Why Do Mbuti Hunters Use Nets? Ungulate Hunting Efficiency of Archers and Net-Hunters in the Ituri Rain Forest." In *American Anthropologist* 93:680–689, 1991.

Index

Index

ABOUT THE AUTHOR

Onukaba A. Ojo was born in Nigeria on March 9, 1960.
He received a Bachelor of Arts in Theatre Arts from the University of Ibadan, Nigeria, in 1982, and a Master of Arts in Journalism from New York University, New York, in 1991. He recently received a Ph.D. from the Department of Performance Studies, Tisch School of the Arts, New York University. He worked as a journalist with *The Guardian Newspapers* in Nigeria from 1983 to 1989.

Ojo is the author of *In the Eyes of Time*, a biography of the Nigerian leader Olusegun Obasanjo. His plays have been produced by the BBC in London.

PHOTO CREDITS

Cover Photo by Eliot Elisofon, National Museum of African Art, Eliot Elisofon Photographic Archives, Smithsonian Institution; all other photos by Dr. Colin M. Turnbull, Joseph Allen Towles Collection, Avery Research Center for African American History & Culture, College of Charleston, Charleston, South Carolina.